FREEMASONS' HALL

*The Home and Heritage
of the Craft*

Took Tour on Tuesday
3-18-03 LAST Day I was
in London

Jack Marchini

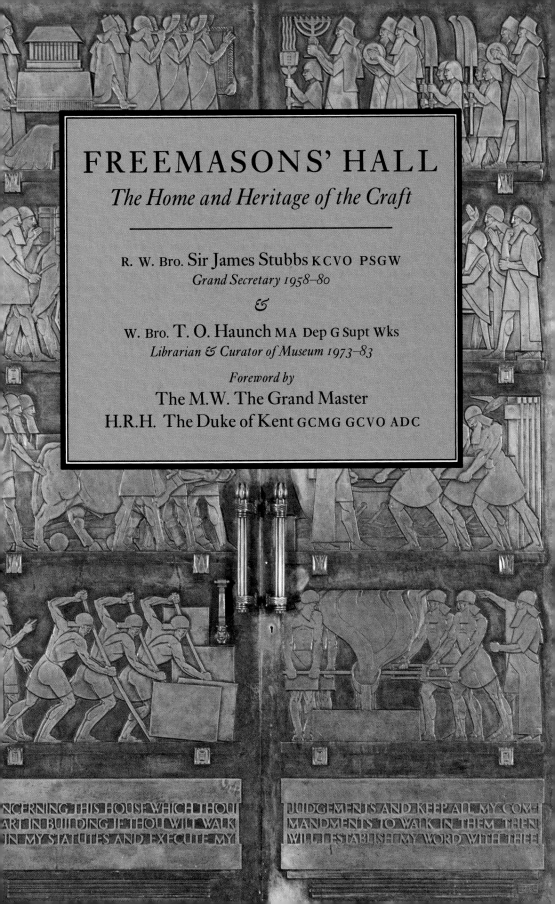

FREEMASONS' HALL

The Home and Heritage of the Craft

R. W. Bro. Sir James Stubbs KCVO PSGW
Grand Secretary 1958–80

&

W. Bro. T. O. Haunch MA Dep G Supt Wks
Librarian & Curator of Museum 1973–83

Foreword by
The M.W. The Grand Master
H.R.H. The Duke of Kent GCMG GCVO ADC

First published 1983 by
The Library, Art and Publications Committee
under the authority of
The Board of General Purposes of
The United Grand Lodge of England

Softback ISBN 0 901075 08 6
Hardback ISBN 0 901075 09 4

Printed in England by
Westerham Press

For over two hundred years Freemasons' Hall in Great Queen Street, has been the focus of English Freemasonry and of regularly organised Freemasonry which spread from English origins throughout the world.

The Freemasons' Hall, which now stands on the site of the buildings of Thomas Sandby and Sir John Soane, and the treasures which it contains, are symbols of the way in which the Craft of Freemasonry has influenced men's lives over two and a half centuries. Together, the building and its contents constitute a continuing account of the life of the Craft.

This book gives a brief insight into that history and an impression of how it is reflected in the building and its contents. I am sure that the book will appeal to and be enjoyed by every Freemason under the United Grand Lodge of England and to others who are interested in Freemasons' Hall and what it stands for.

I congratulate the authors on their enterprise, and commend their work.

Grand Master

The Goose and Gridiron Alehouse, the first meeting place of Grand Lodge, 24 June 1717. Artist's impression based on a sketch published in 1894 when the building was demolished.

Early Meeting Places of Grand Lodge

1717–1776

HE GRAND LODGE OF ENGLAND, the emier Grand Lodge of the world, was ought into being on 24th June (St. John e Baptist's Day) 1717, at an Assembly and east held at the Goose and Gridiron Ale- ouse in St. Paul's Church Yard in the City London. The Goose and Gridiron is no nger in existence, having been demolished 1894, but it stood in London House Yard, alley off the north-west corner of St. ul's Church Yard, in the area that is now ternoster Square and to its south side, here the office building Juxon House now inds.

For the next sixty years Grand Lodge held its ordinary meetings in various inns, taverns and City Livery Company halls. The Annual Assembly and Feast, or Grand Festival as it would now be called, normally took place at the hall of one of the Livery Companies of the City of London, the first such occasion being the installation of the first noble Grand Master, the Duke of Montagu, at Stationers' Hall, in 1721. Thereafter Grand Lodge met for the Annual Assembly in eight other halls, more times than any in that of the Merchant Taylors. It is, indeed, with the record of a meeting in this hall that the first Minute Book of Grand Lodge opens on 23rd June 1723.

In the course of time the desirability and convenience of the Society's having a hall of

icket of Admission to the Grand Festival at the end of the year of office as Grand Master of Thomas, d Viscount Weymouth. One of the earliest engraved masonic documents in the Grand Lodge llection. Dr. Edward Hody, MD FRS, whose signature as Grand Steward is appended to the ticket, is later (1745–6) Deputy Grand Master.

7

Free Masons Tavern in an engraving published in 1784. The first Freemasons' Hall lay to the rear of the Tavern and was approached through the doorway on the right. The Tavern was re-built in 1788–9 to the design pictured on the blue soup plate illustrated on p. 39.

its own must have become apparent. As far as is known the idea was first propounded in public in a speech made by the Junior Grand Warden to the Stewards Lodge in 1763. Certain other proposals were also made at the same time which, after much controversy, came to nothing, but the idea of a Free-masons' Hall survived and in due course came to fruition.

THE GRAND LODGE OF ENGLAND ACCORDING TO THE OLD INSTITUTIONS (the 'Antients' Grand Lodge), during t whole of its existence, from 1751 up to t Union of the two Grand Lodges in 181 never had offices or a permanent meeti place of its own, but met in various inns a taverns in the West End or in the City.

The First Freemasons' Hall
1776

THE FIRST STEPS towards building a hall its own were taken by the Premier Gra Lodge on 28th October 1768, during t Grand Mastership of the Duke of Beaufo when it adopted a plan put forward by t Committee of Charity for 'the most effect Means for raising a Fund to build a Hall a

8

*Robert Edward, 9th Lord Petre, Grand Master 1772–6,
under whose auspices the first Freemasons' Hall was built.
Engraving by A. Freschi
after a portrait by George Romney.*

purchase Jewels, Furniture, &c., for the Grand Lodge.' The Regulations drawn up for this purpose saw the beginning of the system of registration of members and the institution of a scale of Grand Lodge dues.

Little more was achieved for some years until in 1772 Robert Edward, 9th Lord Petre, became Grand Master and actively interested himself in the project. It is noteworthy that its realisation, which was such a milestone in the history of the Grand Lodge of England, should have owed so much to the interest, personal participation and financial support of Lord Petre, one of the three brethren of the Roman Catholic faith who have presided over the Craft as Grand Master.

A committee was appointed 'to consider of, and promote to the utmost of their power the plan for Building a Hall,' and in due course premises in Great Queen Street were purchased for 3,000 guineas (£3,150). They were at No. 61, the frontage lying between what is today the eastern end of Freemasons' Hall and the main entrance to the Connaught Rooms, and they consisted of a 'Front House' on the street with another, the 'Back House' to its rear with a small courtyard between the two; behind the houses lay a garden which was to be the site of the first Freemasons' Hall.

Rooms on the upper floors of the houses were adapted as committee rooms and offices and the front house was let to a Brother Luke

The Freemasons' Hall Medal of 1780, design and engraved by Bro. Edward Parker, a profe sional seal maker. The dies were sunk and t medals struck by Lewis Pingo (1743–183c assistant (later chief) engraver to the Roy Mint.

RIGHT: *Frontispiece to the 1784 Book Constitutions. Allegorical plate drawn Giovanni Battista Cipriani and Paul Sand (water colour artist and brother of the arc tect) and engraved by Francesco Bartolozzi a James Fittler. The background of the pictu shows the interior of the first Freemasor Hall. A note gives this 'Explanation of Frontispiece':*

"*T*HE *architectural part represents t inside of FREE-MASONS'-HAl The upper-most figure is TRUTH, holding mirrour which reflects its rays on div ornaments of the Hall, and also on the Glol and other Masonic Furniture and Imp ments of the Lodge. TRUTH is attena by the three Theological Virtues, FAIT HOPE, and CHARITY: under these, GENIUS of MASONRY, commissioned TRUTH and her Attendants, is descend into the Hall, bearing a lighted Torch, she decorated with some of the Masonic Emble and on her arm hangs a ribbon with a Mea pendant, with which she is to invest t GRAND MASTER, in token of the Div approbation of a Building sacred to Char and Benevolence.*''

B. Cipriani & P. Sandby Delin.

F. Bartolozzi & T. Ftler.

Publish'd as the Act directs
By the SOCIETY *of* FREE MASONS
at their HALL *in* GREAT QUEEN STREET LINCOLNS INN FIELDS 1780

11

ABOVE: *The Grand Temple looking to the masonic east (the original Hall as restored following a fire in 1883) shortly before its demolition in 1933. Note the Grand Master's Throne with the statue of the Duke of Sussex in the niche behind and compare with illustrations on pages 44–45 and 62.*

RIGHT: *The second Freemasons' Hall, 186̶ and the adjoining Tavern. The tinted porti̶ still exists today as the Connaught Rooms.*

illy to become the Freemasons' Tavern and ffee House. Reilly was given authority for e Free Masons' Arms [to] be put up as a n with the following motto – "Vide, Audi, ce"', the motto subsequently adopted, in light rearrangement, by the United Grand dge after the Union of 1813.

The design of the Hall was entrusted to homas Sandby (1721–1798) an architect mber of the Craft, who was commissioned build a Hall for the use of this Society' the sum of £3,000. A fund was opened raise the money and subscribers of £25 dges and individual brethren) received in knowledgement a silver medal, specially signed and struck for the purpose. The ndation stone was laid on 1st May 1775 d building work took just over twelve months, the Hall being Dedicated on 23rd May 1776 by the Grand Master in a form of ceremony followed, in its essentials, for the present building a century and a half later. The Hall was simply a hall of assembly and for many years after its opening it was used on a multi-purpose basis for public lettings, often to non-masonic organisations, and many concerts, 'readings and music', dinners and meetings of various sorts took place there. It was not until the premises surrounding it were rebuilt in the 1860s and it became possible to devote the Hall solely to masonic purposes, that it began to be referred to as the 'Grand Temple', at a time when lodge rooms and masonic halls generally were coming to be revered by this designation.

Sandby's Great Hall continued in use

Engraving from the Illustrated London News of 12 June 1869 showing the new banqueting hall Freemasons' Tavern, now the Grand Hall of the Connaught Rooms.

throughout the nineteenth century, forming the nucleus of the new buildings erected in the 1860s (see next section), and remaining until the Masonic Peace Memorial, the Third Freemasons' Hall, was nearing completion in the nineteen-thirties, though for some years the Quarterly Communications of Grand Lodge had not been held in it because the accommodation was inadequate. During the First World War and just after it the nearby Kingsway Hall or Central Hall, Westminster, had begun to be used for some Quarterly Communications and from the middle of 1926 for all of them. In 1932 consideration was given to what was to be done with the old Hall. A structural survey had revealed grave defects in the fabric of the one hundred and fifty years old building and the Board of General Purposes reluctantly reported to Grand Lodge that 'while fully sharing the general regret which will be felt by the Craft

at the disappearance of a structure with many Masonic associations' it felt bound recommend its demolition, and this, in d course, was started on 28th December 193

On the site so cleared much needed exte sions to the Connaught Rooms were bu including the Balmoral Room and the flo above it. The Balmoral Room, which lies the other side of the light well from, a parallel to, the Grand Lodge Library, is tl today in virtually the same position, and the same level, as the historic Freemaso Hall of 1776.

The Second Freemasons' Hall 1869

VARIOUS ALTERATIONS and extensions the original buildings were carried out in first half of the nineteenth century, nota

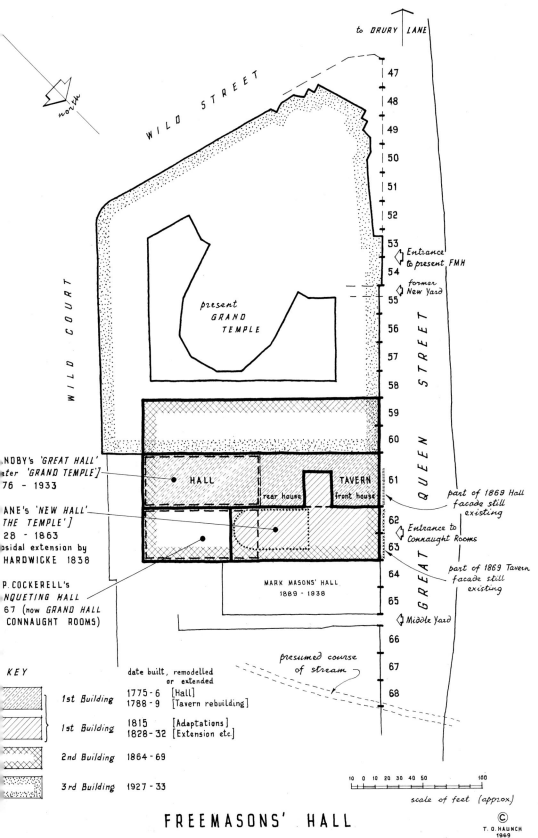

to DRURY LANE

WILD STREET

north

| 47
| 48
| 49
| 50
| 51
| 52
| 53

⇦ Entrance to present FMH

| 54

⇦ former New Yard

| 55

present GRAND TEMPLE

| 56
| 57
| 58
| 59
| 60

QUEEN STREET

WILD COURT

| 61

HALL   TAVERN

rear house   front house

part of 1869 Hall facade still existing

| 62

⇦ Entrance to Connaught Rooms

| 63

part of 1869 Tavern facade still existing

| 64

MARK MASONS' HALL 1889 - 1938

| 65

⇦ Middle Yard

| 66

GREAT

| 67

presumed course of stream

| 68

SANDBY's 'GREAT HALL' [later 'GRAND TEMPLE'] 1776 - 1933

SOANE's 'NEW HALL' ['THE TEMPLE'] 1828 - 1863 apsidal extension by P. HARDWICKE 1838

F. P. COCKERELL's BANQUETING HALL 1867 (now GRAND HALL CONNAUGHT ROOMS)

KEY

	date built, remodelled or extended	
1st Building	1775 - 6	[Hall]
	1788 - 9	[Tavern rebuilding]
1st Building	1815	[Adaptations]
	1828 - 32	[Extension etc.]
2nd Building	1864 - 69	
3rd Building	1927 - 33	

10 0 10 20 30 40 50   100

scale of feet (approx)

FREEMASONS' HALL
COMPOSITE BLOCK PLAN OUTLINING SUCCESSIVE DEVELOPMENTS

© T. O. HAUNCH 1969

by Sir John Soane, the first Grand Superintendent of Works and his successor, Philip Hardwick, but by the middle of the century the hotch-potch of these several developments surrounding the original Hall and extending into adjoining premises had become so inconvenient, and the accommodation so unsatisfactory with the masonic and tavern portions inextricably interlocked, that in 1869 it was decided to undertake a comprehensive rebuilding. The nucleus of Sandby's 'Great Hall' of 1776 would be retained but entirely separate premises provided for public use (i.e. the Tavern) so that the remainder could be devoted solely to masonic purposes and be 'perfectly adapted in all its internal arrangements to the wants of the Brethren, and in its external appearance be ornate in design and creditable to the Order'.

The foundation stone of the new building was laid by the Earl of Zetland with masonic ceremonial on the occasion of the Annual Grand Festival on 27th April 1864 and building work continued over the next five years. The Inauguration of this second Freemasons' Hall eventually took place on 14th April 1869 and 'one of the great objects in building a new Hall being to provide a proper and dignified home for English Freemasonry which should be entirely unconnected with Tavern or Tavern influence' had finally been achieved. This had been effected by disentangling the two functions on plan and by giving each element a distinctive architectural treatment on elevation. Thus Freemasons' Hall itself, at last with its own frontage on Great Queen Street, had a façade in classical style faced with stone whilst the adjoining, but now quite separate, Tavern was built in a harmonising style in brickwork with stone facings. The effect can still be judged from those parts of the 1869 buildings which remain today: the eastern wing of the Hall, now incorporated in the Connaught Rooms as the bay to the right as one faces the main entrance, with Composite columns and pila-

sters, classical statuary and (at roof level) the lower angle of the former central pediment; also, over the entrance to the Connaught Rooms, the original brickwork façade (now painted over) of the 1869 Tavern portion. The main internal feature of the latter was the large banqueting hall adjacent to Sandby's Hall of 1776, designed in Victorian high baroque by Frederick Pepys Cockerell (183.. 1878) the architect for the complex as a whole, and now the Grand Hall of the Connaught Rooms.

Thirty years later the second Freemasons' Hall was extended westwards when (in 189.. two adjoining houses were demolished and rebuilt, the façade of this new wing being treated to match that of the Tavern to the east so that the block of buildings formed a balanced and symmetrical whole. The principal use for this extension was to provide space for the Library and Museum of Grand Lodge which hitherto had lacked accommodation specifically designated for it. Finally, at the end of 1909, the Freemasons' Tavern became dignified by the changing of its name to 'The Connaught Rooms, Freemasons' Hall' in honour of the then Grand Master, the Duke of Connaught and Strathearn.

The Present Freemasons' Hall

SHORTLY BEFORE the outbreak of the First World War further expansion of Freemasons' Hall had been in the air; it was to be a memorial to Edward VII who, as Prince of Wales, had been Grand Master from 1874 to 1901. Money had been collected since 19.. for the purpose by means of a small levy on all members of the Craft. War had prevented the execution of the plan and the stage was set after the cessation of hostilities for a much more thoroughgoing operation. It was therefore decided to pull down and start again financing the project on a voluntary basis with an appeal for funds for the erection of

ABOVE: *The ceremonial laying of the foundation stone of the present Freemasons' Hall by the
Grand Master, the Duke of Connaught, in the
presence of some 8,000 brethren in the Royal
Albert Hall, 14 June 1927, the actual stone being
simultaneously lowered into position on site.*

BELOW: *Three Royal Brothers arriving for the
dedication of the Masonic Peace Memorial on*
*19 July 1933. Leading is the Prince of Wales
(later Edward VIII and subsequently Duke of
Windsor), Provincial Grand Master for Surrey;
beyond him, facing the other way, is the Duke of
York (later George VI), Provincial Grand
Master for Middlesex, and following them is the
Duke of Kent, Senior Grand Warden (later
Provincial Grand Master for Wiltshire and
subsequently Grand Master, 1939–42).*

The Masonic Million Memorial Fund Commemorative jewel issued to individual subscribers.

The design was described at the time as follows:

"The jewel is in the form of a cross, symbolising Sacrifice, with a perfect square at the four ends, on the left and right squares being the dates 1914–1918, the years in which the supreme sacrifice was made. Between these is a winged figure of Peace presenting the representation of a Temple with special Masonic allusion in the Pillars, Porch and Steps. The medal is suspended by the Square and Compasses, attached to a ribband, the whole thus symbolising the Craft's gift of a Temple in memory of those brethren who gave all for King and Country, Peace and Victory, Liberty and Brotherhood."

completely new building to be known (as 1919 and for some years after it was) as Masonic Peace Memorial. There was so debate as to whether it should be on the where its predecessors had been for 150 ye or transferred to the Embankment, but se ment went hand in hand with conservati and with convenience with the result t this, which is in effect the third Freemaso Hall, is still in Great Queen Street.

It will be sufficient here to mention major stages of development: the mess from the Grand Master to the Craft a special meeting for the celebration of pea 27th July 1919, asking for consideration be given to the creation of a perpetual me orial by erecting in 'this Metropolis of Empire' a central home for Freemason the laying of the foundation stone on 1 June 1927, by remote control from a spe meeting at the Royal Albert Hall; the dedi tion of the new building on 19th July 1933

The Masonic Million Memorial Fund flected in its title the target of the appeal a although in the end the building had c appreciably more than the one million pou originally estimated, and although it some years before it was used to its utm capacity from the point of view of maso meetings, the new Hall soon lost its detract and the disappearance in war and peace many old established meeting places ensured that from 1940 onwards it has alw been fully occupied.

The visitor to the Hall will have his inter concentrated on the great ceremonial su and the Library and Museum on the fi floor, for the rest of the building will generally be seen by him unless he has bu ness with the Grand Secretary's office o attending a Lodge or Chapter meeting. It n be of interest, however, briefly to descr the building as a whole before passing or deal in detail with the first floor.

The shape of Freemasons' Hall on pla that of an irregular hollow pentagon,

e (at the junction of Great Queen Street
d Wild Street) being very much fore-
ortened, almost to a point, at the cere-
onial entrance above which rises the tower.
om this point the main axis of the building
ds back to bisect the central open space,
th the Grand Temple block dividing this
o two courts between the surrounding
rimeter blocks. These consist of five main
reys on which, together with the area
low the Grand Temple, accommodation is
posed as follows:—

sement. This is at courtyard level: it con-
ns not only the boilers and other engineer-
; and electrical equipment and workshops,
ether with rooms for maintenance staff,
t also strongrooms, filing and muniment
oms which are essential for the efficient
nning of the Grand Secretary's office as
e nerve centre of Freemasonry.

ound Floor. This contains the accommoda-
n for the Grand Secretary and his Staff,
e Grand Tyler's office which deals with the
ting of lodge rooms, a dispatch office for
and Lodge publications and, not least im-
rtant, an Enquiry Office much used by
itors from the English and other Constitu-
ns. The Board of General Purposes' Room
d its ancillary Committee Rooms are also
this floor, as is the largest Lodge Room
o. 1) containing the principal collection of
rtraits (see page 56).

st Floor. This holds the Library and
useum, a Smoking Room, three Confer-
ce Rooms and the whole Grand Temple
mplex, which are described in detail on
osequent pages.

ond and Third Floors. These are occupied
sixteen self-contained Lodge Room suites
widely varying sizes for the equally varying
quirements of the tenant Lodges and
apters.

zzanine Floor. This is situated between
rt of the ground and first floors and pro-
es two further small Lodge Rooms (bring-
the total in the building to nineteen) and

rooms for use by Lodges of Instruction.
There are also several other small rooms
elsewhere in the building providing for lodge
committees, audit meetings and the like.

Quatuor Coronati Lodge. The secretariat of
the research lodge, Quatuor Coronati No.
2076, and its world-wide Correspondence
Circle, is located in offices on the lower
ground floor of Freemasons' Hall where
members can be given guidance on matters
associated with the Lodge and its publications
in distinction from the more general assis-
tance on the many aspects of Freemasonry
that is always available to all members of the
Craft from the Grand Lodge Librarian and
Curator and his staff.

Library & Museum

THE VISITOR TO Freemasons' Hall wishing
to see something of the building, or seeking advice and information connected with
masonic research (but not on matters of current procedure or administration which are
dealt with by the appropriate department of
the Grand Secretary's Office) will be directed
to the Library and Museum on the first floor.
From the entrance hall in Great Queen Street
this is reached by a pair of lifts or by the
main staircase which lands on the first floor
opposite the Smoking Room. A right turn
from the head of the stairs (left from the
lifts) leads along a corridor past the Library
and Museum Extension, right again past
three Conference Rooms and so into the
main Library and Museum.

The formation of a masonic library for the
United Grand Lodge of England was first
proposed in 1837 but little was done to further the project until towards the end of last
century since which time the Library and
Museum has been built up into the finest and
most comprehensive masonic collection to
be found anywhere. It is today the national
institution in its own subject field and has

established a high reputation both in this country and internationally not only for the scope and quality of its contents but also for the service it can offer to the Craft in general as a centre for information and research, for the identification of artefacts connected with the Order, etc. The Library and Museum also issues a series of information leaflets on a number of subjects about which queries are most frequently received and these are added to from time to time. It should be mentioned at this point that the Library does not maintain a loan collection since so many of its contents are valuable and irreplaceable, and it therefore functions as a reference library only.

The Library, looking towards the Museum. The show-cases down the centre display items recently acquired by the Library and Museum. The long-case clock on the left dates from about 1800 and was made by John Barraclough, of Haworth, Yorkshire, a member of a lodge there.

Library

In addition to an unrivalled collection literature in many languages on every fa of Freemasonry in its various degrees a orders the Library also houses the archi of the United Grand Lodge, the Suprem Grand Chapter and those of a number older and more historically important priv lodges and of others that have gone out existence. These archives form a unique ser of chronicles recording the rise and progre of the world's first Grand Lodge. Th include the Minute Books of the Prem Grand Lodge of 1717 (dubbed by its la rival as 'Modern Masons'), the first of whi opens on the 24th June 1723, six years after founding, those of the 'Antients' Grand Loc of 1751, the Membership Registers of b (from 1768 in the case of the Premier Gra Lodge and from 1751 for the 'Antient early returns and correspondence from lod and many other sources (dating from, rough

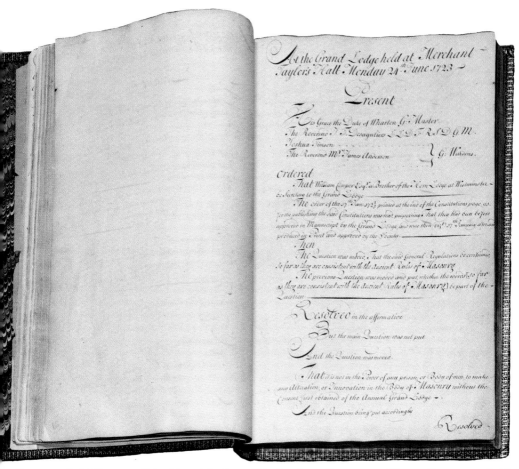

The first recorded Minutes of the Grand Lodge of England, 24 June 1723. The earlier pages of this Minute Book contain lists of lodges and (for the most part) the names of their members.

---

last quarter of the 18th century), Letter Books of the Premier Grand Lodge (from 1768, but with an unfortunate, and for the masonic historian a calamitous gap between 1790 and 1818), and a whole series of assorted registers, committee books, ledgers, notebooks and the like in which are recorded such things as the issue of deputations, warrants and patents of appointment, petitions for relief, lists of lodges, and so on. Such records exist, and are carefully preserved, in respect of the two 18th century Grand Lodges and of the United Grand Lodge into which, after sixty years of dissension and rivalry, they came together on 27th December 1813. The 'Articles of Union', by which this merger was happily effected, is one of the most notable

documents still preserved in the Library. The Royal Arch, too, is represented in a series of records similar to those of the Craft and dating from 1766 when the 'Grand and Royal Chapter of the Royal Arch of Jerusalem' was established by 'Moderns' masons owing allegiance to the Premier Grand Lodge. The 'Charter of Compact' the document which 'instituted and erected' this, the first Grand Chapter, may also be seen in the Library.

Some of the Library's unique and most valuable possessions date from many years before the organisation of free and accepted masonry under a Grand Lodge. These are copies of the *MS. Constitutions,* commonly called the 'Old Charges', of the operative stonemasons. At the present day close on a

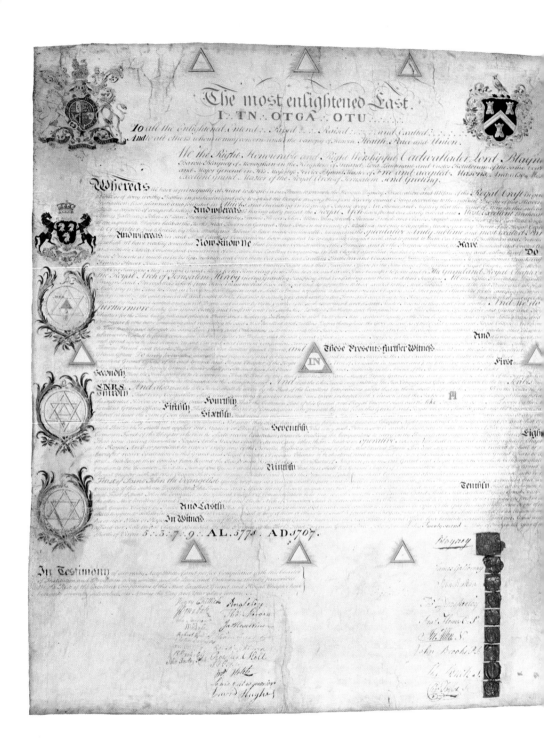

The 'Charter of Compact' by which the first Grand and Royal Chapter of the Royal Arch Jerusalem was instituted in 1766. The dates which appear on the Charter were a later falsification (reference on p.63). The Charter embodies, among other things, the first Regulations about Royal Ar regalia.

THE ARTICLES OF UNION BY WHICH
THE UNITED GRAND LODGE OF ENGLAND
WAS ESTABLISHED.

ABOVE: The inscription on the title page of the Articles, the whole document being finely engrossed on vellum and cased in a richly embroidered binding.

BELOW: The first and last pages of the draft of the Articles as signed at Kensington Palace on 25 November 1813 by the respective Grand Masters, Edward, Duke of Kent for the 'Antients' and Augustus Frederick, Duke of Sussex for the 'Moderns', and other leaders of the Craft on the two sides.

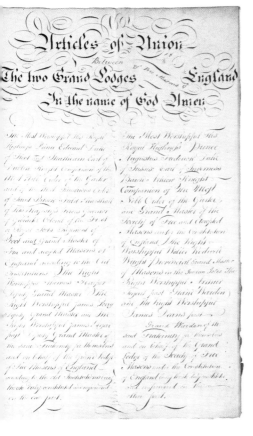

hundred manuscript versions are known to exist (others are now missing, later ones are in engraved or printed form) and of that number the Grand Lodge Library owns, or has custody of forty, some in the form of parchment rolls, others in book form. Whilst the two oldest known versions of the 'Old Charges' are in the British Museum (the *Regius MS.* of c.1390 and the *Cooke MS.* of c.1410), this Library has the next oldest, the *Grand Lodge MS. No. 1*, a narrow vellum roll nearly nine feet (2.75 metres) long which is the oldest of *any* bearing a date, the scribe who copied it out having dated it at the sam time – 25th December 1583.

Apart from these important and irreplac able archives, in which the origins and histo of organised Freemasonry have their roo the major part of the Library comprises, is to be expected, collections of books a manuscripts. In addition to masonic liter ture, there is an extensive and diverse sectie (housed in the Extension) on subjects relate to Freemasonry and others of a more gener nature, many of these being antiquari works of great interest in themselves. On t

BELOW: *The Free-Mason's Calendar. Seven examples from a collection of specially bound copies, in different bindings for each year, and all bearing the bookplate of the Carlton House Library. Those illustrated are for the years 1792, 1793, 1794 (above) and 1797, 1808, 1810 and 1811 (below).*

RIGHT: *The Second Minute Book of Gra Lodge covering the period 1731 to 1771. This the "new Grand Lodge Book" referred to the Minutes for 29 January 1731 as havi been presented by the 8th Duke of Norfe (Grand Master 1730–31) together with t "Sword of State" illustrated on p.47.*

masonic side the Library concerns itself with the Craft throughout the world: not only the English, Irish and Scottish Constitutions but also Commonwealth jurisdictions and those of foreign countries with which the United Grand Lodge of England is in fraternal communication (and of some, indeed, with which it is no longer in amity); these are represented by official and semi-official publications forming an important central reference archive.

The large collection of masonic literature is remarkable for its diversity and comprehensiveness, covering every aspect of Freemasonry written about in this country and in many other parts of the world. It ranges from general masonic history, through the government and organisation of the fraternity to the philosophy of Freemasonry, its symbolism, ritual and ceremonial, its outward and visible signs, its emblems and regalia. Whilst the greater part is devoted to the Craft and Royal Arch, which alone in the English system comprise 'pure Antient Masonry', the many additional degrees and orders also find a place.

Many notable examples of fine 18th and 19th century bindings are to be found in the Library on, for example, Bibles, the large folio Minute Books of the Grand Lodges, their Membership Registers, early editions of the *Constitutions, Freemasons' Calendars* of the late 1700s and early 1800s, and masonic handbooks and general works. Several bindings are by named or known bookbinders and include a number of the distinctive designs of John Lovejoy, a famous exponent of his craft at the end of the 18th century.

Mention must also be made of the enormous collections of prints and documents which the Library houses: prints, engravings, pictures, charts, drawings, photographs etc. of persons and all manner of things and occasions masonic, together with a comprehensive collection, running into several thousands, of warrants, charters, patents of appointment, certificates and other documents covering many degrees and many constitutions.

The contents of the Library are arranged countries or territories, corresponding to the way in which Freemasonry itself is organised and administered, and within these geographical divisions the contents are arranged and catalogued on the same classification scheme.[1] On the main floor level, after reference section and ones devoted to general masonic literature, there are others dealing with all aspects of Freemasonry in England followed in turn by those concerned similarly with Ireland, Scotland and Commonwealth countries. The latter continue in the Library gallery and after them follow the sections covering the Craft in foreign countries.

The showcases down the centre of the Library contain a selection of items recently acquired by the Library and Museum and these, with occasional special exhibitions arranged there, lead the visitor into the Museum proper.

[1]Specially devised to meet the needs of the Grand Lodge Library and Museum by W.Bro. A.R. Hewitt FLA, PJGD, its Librarian and Curator from 1960 1972.

ABOVE RIGHT: *Patent of Appointment of John Allen as Provincial Grand Master for Lancashire 1769. One of the earliest Patents in the Grand Lodge collection.*

BELOW RIGHT: *Petition from Michael Devon "Deputy Secretary to the Grand Lodge", the Deputy Grand Master seeking to enlist help in obtaining employment. From 1758 1769 the Minutes of Grand Lodge were written up by Michael Devon in a similar decorated style. Lodge Warrants issued during this period were also handsomely engrossed by him and could be had either on parchment at half-a-guinea (52½ pence) or "drawn with the usual [masonic] embellishments on Vellum" at five guineas (£5.25).*

LEFT: *One of the four Membership Registers of the Premier Grand Lodge, 1768–1813, in a binding bearing the label of "Brother Willm. Harris, No. 70 St. Paul's Churchyard".*

BELOW: *left to right: Bible in a masonic binding by John Lovejoy (c.1749–1818), believed to be that used at the "Grand Assembly of Freemasons on the Union of the Two Grand Lodges on St. John's Day, 27th December 1813".*

1784 Book of Constitutions in a signed binding by Henry Walther who worked in London c.1770–c.1830. The evidence of this example of his masonic work has enabled a number of unsigned bindings, principally the same edition of the Book of Constitutions and some Bibles, to be attributed to Walther.

1784 Book of Constitutions in a signed binding by John Lovejoy (in a dedication panel on the back). Lovejoy was a member of a number of London lodges and probably the finest finisher of bindings in a masonic style. His work in this field appears principally on Bibles, copies of the 1784 Book of Constitutions and various editions of William Preston's Illustrations of Masonry.

Museum

he Museum, and the Extension to the ibrary and Museum passed on the way in, ntain the Grand Lodge's unique collection regalia, jewels and ceremonial paraphern- ia, masonic silver, porcelain and pottery, assware, furniture and a large range of ndry other objects, extraordinary in their riety, connected with the Craft. On the ain floor of the Museum, in addition to e general displays, the regalia, jewels etc. the English Craft are exhibited together ith those of the several additional masonic grees and orders practised in this country. a territorial arrangement similar to that of e Library the Museum Gallery continues ith those of Ireland and Scotland and rious foreign Grand Lodges, some from untries in which Freemasonry no longer rvives.

The displays of masonic aprons, jewels c., and the portraits of masons in regalia to be seen in the Museum illustrate the great diversity in the design of masonic clothing before the introduction of standard patterns which, for the English Constitution, followed in 1815 after the Union of the two Grand Lodges. There are examples of aprons in a variety of shapes and materials dating from the late 18th and early 19th centuries, with designs hand-drawn and painted, embroi- dered, or engraved and coloured; some of the latter printed types have engraved designs which occur elsewhere as transfers on pottery. Of even greater diversity are the personal jewels of the same period some, in silver, elaborately engraved or fretted with

The Museum, housing the main collections of plate, glassware, porcelain and pottery, jewels and regalia. The 'Sussex Plate' (illustrated on p.33) is seen at the far end. The standards hanging from the gallery balustrades are the personal standards of former Grand Masters.

James Asperne, 1737–1820. Portrait in oils by Samuel Drummond, ARA, 1813. Asperne, bookse.
and stationer, and latterly proprietor of the European Magazine, is shown wearing a Grand Stewar
apron and a Master's chain and jewel; he has the 'Royal Medal' of the Lodge of Antiquity, N
(now No. 2) on his breast and in his right hand is holding a copy of the 1784 Book of Constitutions.

...nall portrait of an unknown mason, c.1820, ...aring a 'gallows pattern' Past Master's jewel ...milar to the example from the Grand Lodge ...llection illustrated on the right. This type of ...vel was current in the first quarter of the 19th ...ntury.

emblems connected with the Craft and associated degrees and known as 'plate' and 'pierced' jewels, others delicately enamelled and enriched with settings of paste brilliants. Such jewels were either badges of office, presentation pieces or were simply worn in lodge by masons as personal adornment. The Museum also holds an enormous and ever-growing collection of lodge jewels, the descendants of those earlier personal jewels, in the form of the consecrating officers', founders', past masters', and the special centenary and members' jewels of private lodges. Only a small representative selection of these is on display but a register is maintained listing all English lodges and chapters and recording what jewels associated with them are held in the reserve collection. This register is openly available for reference by visitors. As with the lodge jewels only a small selection of early festival stewards' jewels of the masonic

charitable institutions are shown but complete sets are held.

The Museum's collection of plate includes many fine specimens of the gold and silversmith's craft, many in the form of commemorative, presentation or association pieces. One of the most impressive and elaborate among these is the large silver centrepiece known as the 'Sussex Plate' from its having been presented to the Duke of Sussex by the Fraternity in 1838 to commemorate his completion of twenty-five years as first Grand Master of the United Grand Lodge of England. It was given back to Grand Lodge by his widow, the Duchess of Inverness, shortly after his death five years later. Additional items in silver and silver gilt such as candelabra, epergnes, cups, salvers, tableware, ceremonial trowels, etc. are exhibited in both the main Museum and the Extension.

Four aprons from the Museum's large collection. Before the introduction of regulation patterns of regalia in 1815 there was a great diversity in such items. Often designed according to the owner's fancy aprons were made from a variety of materials and were hand drawn, painted, embroidered, or printed from engraved plates and were decorated with all manner of emblems, allegorical figures, etc.

'Sussex Plate'. This magnificent silver centre-piece, made by Robert Garrard of London, was presented by the Fraternity to the Duke of Sussex in 1838 to commemorate his completion of twenty- years as Grand Master of the United Grand Lodge. It was later returned to Grand Lodge by his dow. The centre-piece is slightly over one metre in height and just under one metre across.

ABOVE: *A selection of 18th and early 19th century plate and pierced jewels, lodge officers' and R*
Arch jewels.

BELOW: *A small selection from the huge number of enamel and paste jewels held in the Museum, th*
illustrated being presentation pieces (often with allegorical figures), personal or lodge members' jew
Note particularly, bottom row second from right, the silver, paste and enamel jewel presented
Anthony Ten Broeke, Master of Caledonian Lodge (now) No. 134, in 1768. The portrait of
reproduced opposite shows him wearing this jewel.

nthony Ten Broeke. Portrait in oils by an unknown artist, c.1768. Ten Broeke was a member of ledonian Lodge, No. 325 (now No. 134) in 1763 and its Master in 1766. The ornamental Master's lar in silver chain-work which he is wearing is still worn by the W.M. of Caledonian Lodge. The r-shaped jewel above it was presented to Ten Broeke by the Lodge in 1768 and is now in the Museum lection; it is among those illustrated opposite.

A SELECTION OF SILVERWARE OF THE
18th, 19th AND PRESENT CENTURIES.

LEFT: *Two handled cup and cover by Ebenezer
Coker, London, 1774. Presented on 27 December
1826 to W.Bro. James Ames, Master of the
Lodge of Innocence and Morality, No. 592,
Hindon, Wiltshire (erased 1832) by the members
of the Lodge ''as a token of their Esteem for the
Zeal and Fidelity with which during 30 Years
he presided over it.''*
CENTRE: *Silver presentation piece in the form
of a cradle, Birmingham, 1901. Presented to the
wife of W.Bro. Gordon de Lacy Larner by the
members of Holloway Lodge, No. 2601, ''to
mark the happy event of the birth of a daughter
during his term of office as Worshipful Master,
18 September 1901.''*
RIGHT: *Pair of Swedish silver candlesticks
presented by the Grand Lodge of Sweden on the
250th Anniversary of the Grand Lodge of
England, 1967.*

FOREGROUND: *Trowel used for the la[y]
with masonic ceremonial, of the Founda[tion]
Stone of the Shakespeare Memorial The[atre]
Stratford-upon-Avon, 2 July 1929, by the
Grand Master, Lord Ampthill. Designed [and]
made at the Stratford-upon-Avon Schoo[l of]
Art.*

*French silver wine taster, late 18th cent[ury]
decorated on the base with the square and c[om]
passes and letter 'G' within a five-pointed st[ar].*

*Silver plated sweetmeat dish engraved [with]
the square and compasses and the lodge nu[mber]
'999' (Robert Burns Lodge, Manchester).*

ver gilt cup with cover and plinth, by J. & E. Terry, London, 1836; height 660mm. Presented in 36 by the Masons of Somerset to their Provincial Grand Master, Col. Charles Kemys Kemys-Tynte 779–1860). The handles of the cup are formed by the figures of Faith and Hope and the cover mounted by that of Charity. The decoration on the bowl and base features pomegranates and acacia.

Indian gold and silver casket, by Jellicoe, Calcutta, 1875; 330 × 83 × 83 mm. Made to contain (wh *it still does) an Illuminated Address presented by the Masons of Bengal to the Prince of Wales (la* *Edward VII), M.W.G.M., on his visit to Calcutta in 1875. Presented to the Museum by Her Maje* *The Queen in 1967.*

The porcelain and pottery on display covers a range of styles and periods from exquisite Meissen groups, and punchbowls, tankards, plates etc. in Chinese export porcelain of the Chi'en Lung, 'famille rose' period (1735–1795), to the products of several English potteries for which the discovery in about 1756 of a method of transfer printing on pottery opened the way for large scale manufacture for the masonic, as well as the general market. Examples are to be seen in various showcases of masonic pottery from Worcester and Staffordshire, of Leeds, Liverpool and Wedgwood creamware, and of the ubiquitous Sunderland purple lustreware together with examples from this latter source of the less common silver and yellow lustre pottery.

Porcelain from a few well-known continen factories is also exhibited, as are so examples of English wares of the pres century, including an unrivalled collecti of Goss with masonic devices or armor bearings.

Masonic 'fire', the toasting routine deriv from 18th century drinking customs a masonic table ritual developed in Fran calls for the use of small drinking glasses distinctive pattern with specially enlarg and thickened bases to withstand the rappi upon the table to which they are subject. The Museum has a number of these on sh dating from the late 18th century to m modern examples; some particularly intere ing ones, decorated with coloured enamelli

*eissen porcelain group and figures. Those of men date from the 18th century, the crinoline lady from
e 19th, and are all after models by Johann Joachim Kaendler, the eminent sculptor employed by the
eissen factory in the mid-1700s.*

*me fine examples of masonic porcelain and pottery of the 18th and 19th centuries, including Chinese
port porcelain of the Chi'en Lung period, Worcester (Dr. Wall) pottery, Liverpool creamware,
nderland lustreware, and a Staffordshire soup plate transfer printed in blue with a view of
eemasons' Tavern, c.1790.*

Three masonic firing glasses by William Beilby, of Newcastle-upon-Tyne, the celebrated enameller on flint glass. Beilby (1740–1819), who had learned painting and enamelling in Birmingham, is given credit for being the first to perfect the art of decorating flint glass in colour.

are attributed to William Beilby (1740–1819), of Newcastle-upon-Tyne, who is credited with having first developed this technique of decorating flint glass with coloured enamels. Apart from the many firing glasses, of which only a small selection is on display, the Museum houses also a large and splendid collection of other masonic glassware: goblets, rummers, decanters, carafes, ewers, jugs and drinking glasses and flutes of all shapes and sizes (the hollow bases of some containing a coin or set of dice), many skilfully and pleasingly engraved with a wealth of masonic and other designs, a favourite one being the 'fruiting vine' pattern. The Museum also possesses a few fine examples of Bristol and other blue glassware with masonic decoration.

Interesting relics of masonry in times of war and poignant reminders of what Free-

A selection of 18th and 19th century masonic glassware giving an indication of the great variety of types, styles and sizes, and of the diversity of masonic emblems and other decoration applied to them.

masonry meant to brethren in adversity are seen in displays covering the Napoleonic, South African and First and Second World Wars. They range from collage jewels and plaques made and sold to eke out their existence by French prisoners of war interned in this country in the early 19th century, by way

A fine Bristol blue glass decanter and facetted stopper with gold decoration, c.1770. The front has the Arms of the Premier Grand Lodge and the name 'Lodge of Perfect Union'. This 'Moderns' lodge was constituted in May 1763 and met at the White Hart, High Street, Chippenham, Wiltshire; it was erased from the Roll in 1773. The back shows the commonly occurring masonic motifs of the sun in splendour, the crescent moon and the seven stars; the neck has the 'fruiting vine' pattern.

FREEMASONS UNDER ARMS – *a selection of masonic relics of Wars and Prisoners of War spanning one and a half centuries.*

ABOVE LEFT: *Three jewels of the kind made for sale by French prisoners of war interned in England during the Revolutionary and Napoleonic Wars, 1793–1814. Modelled on the 'plate' jewels then popular with Freemasons any materials that came to hand were used in their manufacture – scraps of bone, mother of pearl, wire and tinsel, paper, painted work etc.*

CENTRE: *Collar and jewel worn as a lodge secretary's badge of office at masonic meetings held throughout the siege of Ladysmith during the South African War, 1899–1900.*

CENTRE LEFT: *Past Master's emblem made from a penny by a British prisoner of war in Oflag 78 in Germany during the Second World War.*

BELOW LEFT: *Working Tools used in a Lodge of Instruction organised by British prisoners of war in a German Oflag in the Second World War. The materials were obtained from the camp beds.*

BELOW CENTRE: *Ritual book used at maso[n]ic meetings in various prisoner of war ca[mps] in Germany, including that mentioned in [the] previous item. The fly leaves and half-title b[ear] the signatures of some of the brethren who t[ook] part.*

ABOVE RIGHT: *Bible used in the Maso[nic] Club held at the River Valley Road prisoners [of] war camp, Singapore.*

BELOW RIGHT: *Lodge Officers' jewels fro[m a] set made by a prisoner of war in Changi J[ail,] Singapore, and used in a lodge that met th[ere] clandestinely. The metal was salvaged from [a] wrecked bus.*

ABOVE CENTRE: *Apron made from a hand-kerchief used at meetings during the siege of Ladysmith.*

ABOVE RIGHT: *Square and Compasses used at meetings in the trenches in Flanders during the First World War. The Square was obtained from a farmer in exchange for food, the Compasses were manufactured by one of the brethren.*

BELOW RIGHT: *Past Master's apron of the Willem van Oranje Lodge formed in 1918 by British Prisoners of war transferred from Germany to the Netherlands under the Hague Convention. On the cessation of hostilities the Lodge was removed to London under the English Constitution and still exists today.*

LEFT: *Apron and badges of rank for Provincial Grand Officers typical of those improvised for the resumption of masonic meetings in Jersey after the liberation of the Channel Islands in 1945.*

BELOW CENTRE: *Portrait medallion of Field Marshal Lord Kitchener of Khartoum, Past Junior Grand Warden.*

of items associated with the South African War and in particular with the siege of Lady-smith, down to our own times and the relics that have survived from German and Japanese prisoner of war camps and the German occupation of the Channel Islands.

The visitor who on his way in reached the main Library and Museum via the Extension cannot fail to have had his attention caught there by the Grand Master's throne with the two Wardens' chairs *en suite*. This set of chairs was made in 1791 shortly after the election as Grand Master of George, Prince of Wales (later Prince Regent and ultimately George IV). They were in regular use in the former Grand Temple (the first Freemasons' Hall described earlier) until the present Freemasons' Hall was brought into use. Every Grand Master since 1791 – ten to date – has been installed in his office on this throne. Several examples of lodge chairs are to be seen elsewhere in the Museum or on the Library gallery, notably some in the style of Hepplewhite and Chippendale and including

Under the immediate recommendation of HIS MOST GRACIOUS MAJESTY WILLIAM the FOURTH, GRAND PATRON.
This Print of H.R.H. Prince Augustus Frederick Duke of Sussex K.G. K.T. K.G.H. &c. &c. &c. M.W. Grand Master.
of the United Free & Accepted MASONS of ENGLAND.
Is most respectfully Inscribed to The Grand Lodge of England, By their most Obed.t Humble & Devoted Serv.t
Brother JOHN HARRIS P.M

ɃOVE: *The Grand Master's Throne and Grand ₁ardens' Chairs made by Robert Kennett, 1791. 𝑟e Ducal Coronet surmounting the Throne 𝑟s substituted for the original Prince of Wales's 𝑟athers (seen in the engraving opposite) when 𝑟 Duke of Connaught became Grand Master 𝑟901. The feathers have not, unfortunately, 𝑟vived.*

ₜFT: *Engraving by John Harris, 1833, of the 𝑢ke of Sussex, sixth son of George III, first 𝑟and Master (1813–1843) of the United 𝑟and Lodge of England. He is shown seated on 𝑟 Grand Master's Throne, seen here in its 𝑖ginal state which may be compared with the 𝑢stration above. John Harris (1791–1873), 𝑐hitectural draughtsman, miniaturist and ex-𝑟t facsimilist, is best known in Freemasonry 𝑟 his designs for Tracing Boards.*

(in the latter style) a fine set on loan to the Museum from Britannic Lodge, No. 33.

The panoply of masonic ceremonial is represented in the Museum by a number of items among which the following are perhaps the most notable: the Grand Lodge Sword, presented in 1730 by the Duke of Norfolk (Grand Master 1730–31), and the Grand Registrar's Bag, made to contain the Articles of Union in 1813, both still carried in the procession into and out of meetings of Grand Lodge; the standard of Grand Lodge and the personal standard of the Grand Master and those of his predecessors since 1874; the Sword of Supreme Grand Chapter, once the ceremonial sword of the 'Antients' Grand Lodge. The connection of the Royal House with English Freemasonry is evidenced by a family tree showing all those members of the Royal Family who have been Freemasons since Frederick Lewis, Prince of Wales (the eldest son of George II) who was made a mason in 1737. Also on exhibition are the masonic regalia, jewels and decorations of

H.R.H. Arthur, Duke of Connaught and Strathearn, KG, Grand Master 1901–1939.
Portrait by Sir Arthur Cope, KCVO RA.

oyal brethren who have been actively con-
ected with the Craft over the last one-and-
half centuries.

In addition to the more important main
asses of exhibits described in the preceding
ges the Grand Lodge Museum also pos-
sses an enormous number of other miscel-
neous items having masonic associations
t to which reference can only briefly be
ade: snuff mulls and snuff-boxes (in silver,
amels, papier mâché etc.), tobacco and
cigarette boxes (from lead to silver and gold),
pipes (from the humble churchwarden to
the noble meerschaum), clocks and pocket
watches (even sundials), fob seals and watch-
chain charms, spirit flasks and wine bottles,
rolling pins and razors, trowels and toasting
forks, door knockers and horse brasses, and
treen in variety. In short, everything from
objects of virtu to masonic bric-à-brac but all
in their diverse ways linking the Craft with
all sorts and conditions of men.

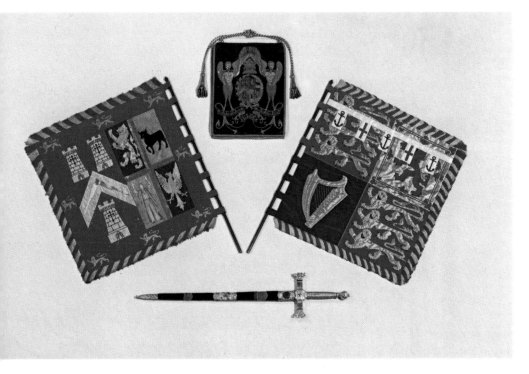

CEREMONIAL INSIGNIA OF GRAND LODGE.

ABOVE: *The richly embroidered Bag of the
Grand Registrar, made to contain the Articles
of Union, 1813 (see text p.21 illustration, p.23).*
LEFT: *The Standard of Grand Lodge bearing
the Arms of the United Grand Lodge of England,
combining those unofficially used by the two
former Grand Lodges, and regularised by a
formal Grant of Arms in 1919 when, to mark
the long association of the Royal House with the
Craft, the 'bordure' with its lions recalling the
Arms of England, was added.*

RIGHT: *The personal Standard of The M.W.
The Grand Master, H.R.H. The Duke of Kent.
The Royal Arms differenced with a label of five
points argent, the first, third and fifth points
each charged with an anchor azure, and the
second and fourth with the Cross of St. George.*
BELOW: *The Grand Lodge Sword of State,
presented to Grand Lodge by the Duke of
Norfolk in 1730. The silver-gilt hilt and the
mountings with masonic embellishments on the
scabbard were made by George Moody, Royal
Armourer and first Grand Sword Bearer of
Grand Lodge, 1733.*

Processional Corridor, looking towards the Grand Officers' Room.

The Ceremonial Suite

ocessional Corridor

OM THE MAIN Museum the visitor enters
range of rooms associated with meetings
the Grand Temple. The first of these is
Grand Officers' Room where those taking
rt in processions robe before assembling in
Processional Corridor. A small suite for
use of the Grand Master and his entourage
ds off the start of this corridor, one side of
ich is flanked by the cloak and robing
ms for Past Grand Officers. The Proces-
nal Corridor is a broad and handsomely
portioned gallery panelled with mahogany
d having a floor of marble and mosaic,
aid with panels of rubber. Stained glass
ndows depicting the four Cardinal Virtues,
ether with a fifth portraying Charity, are
be seen at opposite ends and in the lobby
the farther end. Through this lobby the
ocessional Corridor leads by an awkward
ht-angle bend (well calculated to break
step of any procession) into a vestibule,
immediate ante-chamber to the Grand
mple, and the last of three forming the
in access to the latter.

These three vestibules form a ceremonial
proach to the Grand Temple of increasing
hness in architectural treatment and decora-
n. Separated from each other by two fine
enwork bronze screens, they have walls
d floors lined with marble, and much use is
de of mosaic and colour in the decoration
the floors and ceilings.

st Vestibule

e First Vestibule (i.e. that farthest from
Grand Temple) lies immediately above
Main Entrance at the junction of Great
een Street and Wild Street. It is the setting
the War Memorial Shrine and Window
d serves also as an assembly lobby for
ethren attending meetings in the Grand
mple. On the wall of this vestibule and of
ground floor entrance hall below it are
recorded the names of those Lodges which,
by their support of the Fund for the erection
of the building, qualified for the Hall Stone
Jewel, still worn today by their Master.

The stained glass windows on the winding
staircase leading up on either side from the
general cloak and robing rooms on the ground
floor represent the six periods of Creation.
The uppermost panel in the central window
is reminiscent of William Blake's famous
painting 'The Ancient of Days' and recalls
the well-known passage in Milton's *Paradise
Lost* describing the Creator as the Great
Geometer:

"... and in his hand
He took the golden compasses, prepared
In God's eternal store, to circumscribe
This universe, and all created things."

Memorial Window

The theme of the stained glass Memorial
Window over the Shrine is the attainment of
Peace through Sacrifice. The main feature of
the design is derived from the Commemora-
tive Jewel of the Masonic Million Memorial
Fund, but here the figure of Peace is seen
holding a model of the Tower façade of
Freemasons' Hall (the same figure on the
Hall Stone Jewel itself holds a classical
temple).

Shrine

The Shrine was designed by Bro. Walter
Gilbert[1] and with its two flanking Columns of
Light is a fine example of the bronzeworker's
craftsmanship. The design and ornamenta-
tion incorporate symbols connected with the
theme of Peace and the attainment of Eternal
Life. This symbolism is brought to a focus in
the roundel in the centre of the front of the
Ark, an emblematical reminder that the Soul
of Man rests ultimately in the Hand of his
Creator. This idea is expressed again in the

---

[1]Walter Gilbert (1871–1946), sculptor, metal worker
and designer; executed work for many public buildings,
notably the Great Gates to Buckingham Palace, the
Victoria Memorial facing the Palace, and sculpture in
Liverpool Cathedral.

Memorial Window and Shrine.

ne design on the inner face of the Grand
mple doors.

At the four corners of the Shrine stand
irs of winged Seraphim carrying golden
mpets, and across the front are four gilded
ures portraying Moses the Law Giver,
shua the Warrior High Priest, Solomon
e Wise and St. George of England.

The Roll of Honour of the First World
ar is displayed through an aperture on the
 of the Shrine, guarded by kneeling figures
presenting the fighting Services.

Second Vestibule

The middle vestibule provides an ante-room
in which scrutineers check the credentials of
those seeking admission to meetings of Grand
Lodge, and in which Brethren register their
attendances at these and other meetings.

Third Vestibule

The last of the three halls is the ante-chamber
to the Grand Temple and is the most splendid
of the three in its architectural treatment and
decoration. The richly coloured ceiling con-
trasts with, and is set off by, the plain marble

Ceiling of the Third Vestibule, the ante-chamber to the Grand Temple.

Grand Temple Doors – Inner face.

lls and is echoed in the elaborate floor
ttern in marble and mosaic, with a central
ulti-pointed star inlaid in the semi-
ecious stone, lapis lazuli.

and Temple Doors

he great bronze doors to the Grand Temple,
signed by Bro. Walter Gilbert in con-
nction with the architects, are set in
surround of white statuary marble sur-
ounted by the Arms of the United Grand
dge of England. On either side, within the
rround, is an engaged column, and on the
tel across the head is the Sacred Symbol,
adiated. Each door is cast in one piece and
easures 12 feet by 4 feet (3.66 metres by
2 metres), and each weighs one and a
arter tons.

The reliefs on the outward facing side of
e doors are conventionally pictorial, depic-
g historical events. The three lower panels
each door show scenes connected with
e building of King Solomon's Temple in
rusalem, and the top left and right hand
nels together the procession for the Dedica-
n of the Temple. The inscription at the
ot is God's promise to King Solomon as
corded in the *I Kings, vi. 12.*

The inner face of the doors presents an
ward-looking, mystical and symbolic design,
ll of spiritual significance, in contrast to
e historical themes on the outside. On either
de is a seraph, the great six-winged Sera-
im of the vision of Isaiah (*Isaiah, vi, 2*). At
e top of the left hand leaf is again the
mbol of the Soul of Man resting in the
nd of his Creator, and on the opposite door
e other hand of God holds the Scales to
igh him in the balance. Below these sym-
ls is what the artist called the 'Starry Girdle
Purity', dividing things heavenly from
ose earthly, the latter being represented by
umber of figures denoting various divinely
spired attributes of the human spirit. They
clude two pairs of figures, the one David
d Jonathan (symbolising Brotherly Love),
d the other two soldiers of the First World

Grand Temple Doors – Outer face.

War (symbolising self-sacrifice and echoing
the concept of the building as a War
Memorial).

The Grand Temple

The Grand Temple, the climax of the Ceremonial Suite, is a great meeting hall, 123
feet long, 90 feet wide and 62 feet high
($37 \times 27.5 \times 19$ metres), seating approxi-
mately 1,700 persons. It is used for the five
meetings per year of Grand Lodge (the four
Quarterly Communications and the Annual
Investiture), and for the three Regular Con-
vocations of Supreme Grand Chapter. In
addition the Annual Meetings of a number
of Provincial Grand Lodges of the home
counties and of certain Provincial Grand
Chapters are held in the Grand Temple, as
are also meetings of the Grand Lodge of
Mark Master Masons and those of the Orders
of the Knights Templar and of Malta. No
meetings of private Lodges or Chapters take

Grand Temple from the masonic north west.

place in the Temple except on the occasion of the London Grand Rank Investitures in the Craft and Royal Arch, when the host Lodge or Chapter opens the proceedings before receiving and handing over to the Grand Officers conducting the Investitures.

Walls

The walls of the Grand Temple are faced with Botticino marble with a base of Belgian black marble inlaid with panels of Ashburton. The linings and surrounds to the openings in the corner splay walls are of Alpes Jade marble.

The hangings in the various parts of the Temple are of special design and exceptionally fine quality, particularly those at the back of the dais and in the splay doorways. They are respectively in a gold metal brocade and a heavy silk brocatelle.

The frieze on the four splay walls carries the twelve Signs of the Zodiac. These have no Masonic significance but are a nostalgic link with the two former Freemasons' Ha[ll] which featured them in their decoration, did many other old masonic buildings.

Ceiling

The central panel is a representation of t[he] traditional 'covering' of a Freemasons' Lod[ge] – a 'Celestial Canopy of divers colours, ev[en] the Heavens'. Surrounding it is a deeply c[of]fered and richly decorated border with t[he] Arms of the United Grand Lodge at ea[ch] corner.

Cove

The decoration of the great cove, 15 feet (4 metres) in girth, is entirely in mosaic wo[rk] The allegorical groups in the design ea[ch] incorporate columns of the Classical Ord[er] of Architecture appropriate to its positio[n] They depict respectively:

East. Jacob's Ladder, bearing the symb[ols] for Faith, Hope and Charity, ascending the Sacred Symbol of the Most High. To t[he] left, King Solomon: to the right, King Hira[m]

54

W

E

Grand Temple ceiling.

55

West. Euclid and Pythagoras on either side of the 47th Proposition with the moon overhead.

South. Helios, the Greek sun-god, driving his chariot across the heavens to mark the sun at its meridian.

North. Between the Two Great Pillars the Arms of the Duke of Connaught and Strathearn (the M.W. The Grand Master at the time the Hall was built). In the background, St. George and the Dragon.

Corners. Angelic figures portraying the Four Cardinal Virtues – Prudence, Temperance, Fortitude and Justice.

Inscription. The wording commences in the north-east corner and is taken from *I Chronicles, xvii, 12–14*.

Furniture

The Grand Master's Throne and Pedestal, together with the Chairs of the Deputy and Assistant Grand Masters to the left and right respectively (facing), are of gilt with a covering of fine silk damask. The Wardens' Chairs and Pedestals, designed in keeping with tho[se] on the dais, complete a striking suite of Lod[ge] furniture.

Organ

The console is situated in the centre at t[he] head of the dais. The organ is a three manu[al] Willis instrument with over 2,000 speaki[ng] pipes.

On leaving the Grand Temple, and [by] turning right through a small lobby and rig[ht] again, the visitor will find himself back at t[he] head of the main staircase having complet[ed] a clockwise circuit of the First Floor. In th[us] his time and attention will have been focuss[ed] on the rooms described in the precedi[ng] pages with the Grand Temple as the clim[ax] of his visit, but there are other matters [of] interest which those who have leisure a[nd] inclination may wish to study. As an examp[le] the next section is devoted to a brief revi[ew] of the pictures and statuary to be seen [in] various parts of the Hall.

No. 1 Lodge Room and gallery of portraits of former Grand Masters.

thony Sayer, first Grand Master of the first Grand Lodge of the world. Mezzotint by John Faber
younger, c.1749/50, after a lost portrait by Joseph Highmore. The oval portrait of Sayer seen above
right-hand corner door in the illustration opposite is said to derive from the Highmore original.

Pictures and Statuary

No. 1 Lodge Room was originally intended for meetings of Grand Chapter (for which it was for various reasons quickly found to be quite unsuitable), but in practice it has long been used as an ordinary Lodge Room for larger than normal meetings and as a picture gallery. In it are to be found portraits of all the Grand Masters of the United Grand Lodge from 1813 to 1967, of the Premier Grand Lodge from 1767 to 1813 together with Anthony Sayer and Dr. Desaguliers (the first and third Grand Masters), and of the last two of the 'Antients'. Historically if not always artistically it is a noteworthy collection, which it is not necessary to mention in full detail, as each of the full length portraits carries the name and relevant details on a plaque. It seems likely that the Rev. Matthew William Peters, R.A., (1742-1814) the only holder of the office of Grand Portrait Painter (1785) established the custom of portraying Grand Masters in the Premier Grand Lodge because he was primarily a copyist, and several of the earlier portraits were copies by his own hand. Unhappily the fire by which the Grand Temple was gutted in 1883 destroyed his handiwork and that of other painters, but Grand Lodge employed several copyists as soon as the Grand Temple was available again, and the gaps were filled – at a cost which has been worked out as 150 pence per square foot! The portraits of later Grand Masters are originals, and in most cases of high quality. Most of them are in formal robes, Garter, Thistle and Coronation, but there are six interesting exceptions: Sayer and Desaguliers can lay no claim to be anything but imaginary, though it is said that Sayer's derives at several removes from a lost portrait of him by Joseph Highmore (J.G.W. in 1728); Lord Petre who laid the foundation stone of the first Hall in 1775 is wearing the everyday dress of the time, obviously because, being a Roman Catholic, he was unable to

achieve civil honours and distinctions; t Earl (later Marquess) of Ripon almost exac a century later became a Roman Catho and surrendered the Grand Mastersh though by this time his co-religionists longer suffered the disadvantages of L Petre's generation; the 5th Duke of Beauf (Grand Master, 1767-1771) was missi from the collection until the 10th Duke v kindly, at the behest of the Earl of Scarbrou when Grand Master, presented Grand Loc with a very pleasant half length picture Francis Cotes, R.A., (1726-1770); last there had not been time or opportunity in sadly short Grand Mastership of Geor Duke of Kent, to have a formal portr painted before his death on active service 1942. The Craft was very fortunate in bei able to obtain the charming and natural p traits behind the Master's Chair from N Simon Elwes, who was both a personal frie of the Duke and a wartime patient in t Royal Masonic Hospital.

Besides this picture gallery there are ot rooms which house portraits of varying h torical value. Reference has already be made to those in the Museum of masons regalia but particularly noteworthy also portraits in the Library and Museum Ext sion of the Prince of Wales (later Prir Regent, afterwards George IV). There i fine head and shoulders study by Sir Thon Lawrence, R.A., (1769-1830), on loan fr the Lodge of Antiquity, No. 2, and a fu length portrait of the Prince in Garter rob This is one of a number of copies from studio of Lawrence after the original in own hand, painted circa 1818, in the Ro Collection at Buckingham Palace. In the la Conference Room adjoining the Extensi are representations of Grand Secretaries sii 1769 (excluding the nine who served 'Antients' Grand Lodge); by an unintentior piece of symbolism they are situated in room immediately over the head of the c rent Grand Secretary.

H.R.H. George, Duke of Kent, Grand Master 1939–42.
Portrait by Simon Elwes, ARA.

ABOVE: *H.R.H. Frederick Lewis, Prince of Wales, the first English Royal Freemason, 1737.*
BELOW: *H.R.H. Henry Frederick, Duke of Cumberland, Grand Master 1782–1790, Patron of Grand Chapter 1774–1790. The portrait, doubtfully attributed to John Hoppner, depicts the Duke in Royal Arch regalia.*

In one of the smaller Committee Room on the ground floor is a portrait of an earl Prince of Wales and the first Royal Fre mason, Frederick Lewis, son of George and father of George III, painted by Charl Philips (1708–1747), himself at one time resident of Great Queen Street. Other pair ings in these rooms portray the Duke Cumberland in Royal Arch regalia (Gra Master 1782–1790, and Patron of Gra Chapter 1774–1790), Lord Blayney (Gra Master 1764–1766, and the earliest Fir Grand Principal, 1766–1769), the Duke Richmond (Grand Master, 1724), and fi Presidents of the Board of General Purpos – not, unfortunately, as complete a set the Grand Masters and Grand Secretari Lords Moira, Ampthill and Cornwallis repr sent the Pro Grand Masters and Sir Frederi Halsey the Deputy Grand Masters. T Grand Officers' Room on the first flo has the Prince of Wales (Grand Mast 1874–1901), together with Lords Carnarvo Lathom and Amherst, who functioned Pro Grand Masters during that time.

On the staircase to the Museum galle (and best viewed from the gallery landing) the notable painting 'Joshua commandi the Sun to stand still on Gibeon'[1] by Jo Martin (1789–1854), whose large canvass of cataclysmic scenes drawn from the Bib created sensations when first exhibited.

The Hall is not particularly well off f statuary: the massive statue of the Duke Sussex (ground floor, Board Room corrid is outstanding. It was executed in 1846 Edward Hodges Baily, R.A., (1788–186 who four years earlier had carved the stat of Lord Nelson for the column in Trafalg Square. The busts of the five royal brothe (in the Library and Museum Extension) five of the six sons of George III who we Masons – are more interesting, as compari one with another, than as works of art. Th

[1]see Joshua, x, 12 & 13

H.R.H. George, Prince of Wales
(later Prince Regent and subsequently George IV).
Portrait by Sir Thomas Lawrence, RA,
on loan to the Grand Lodge Library and Museum
from the Lodge of Antiquity, No. 2.

portray George IV, William IV, and the Dukes of York, Kent and Sussex (the set lacks the unpopular Duke of Cumberland – later King of Hanover). The first-named and the last are by Sir Francis Leggatt Chantry, R.A., (1781–1841), the Duke of York by Baily, and William IV and the Duke of Kent by John Francis (1780–1816).

Conclusion

Those who have read thus far, or those who have used this book as a guide to the building, will have realised that the centre point of English Freemasonry has been here for over two centuries: we may add with pride and without undue self-glorification that here has been also the centre point of regular and organised world Freemasonry which sprang from English origins *in fact* – whatever may be the theories and fantasies about the birth of Freemasonry itself.

It should not be necessary to stress the point that Freemasons' Hall is not merely the chief meeting place in London, housing as it does some 800 masonic bodies, or the administrative centre of the United Grand Lodge of England: it is still justly looked upon as the inspiration of regular Free-masonry wherever it is practised all over the world, since English Freemasonry is the touchstone by which the regularity of other Masonic bodies may be, and generally is, tested.

It is appropriate, therefore, that the Mother Grand Lodge of the World should be housed in surroundings which, for dignity and grandeur, have scarcely been equalled and, assuredly, never yet surpassed.

Statue of the Duke of Sussex by Edward Hodg Baily, 1846. This statue originally stood on a s feet high cylindrical stone plinth in a nicl behind the Throne in the old Grand Temple (s illustration on p.12).

BOLTON, ARTHUR T. [ED.]:
The Works of Sir John Soane, FRS FSA
RA (1753–1837). Sir John Soane
Museum Publication No. 8. London,
1923.

CARR, HARRY:
A guided tour of the Grand Lodge
Library and Museum, Freemasons'
Hall, London. AQC Vol. 78 (1965).

[CHILTON, H. F. D.]
The Doors of the Temple. Masonic
Record, March 1949.
The Windows. Masonic Record, May
1949.
[H. F. D. Chilton was Assistant
Curator of Grand Lodge, 1946–63; his
articles under the pseudonym John
Smith are essays on the symbolism of
the features referred to in their titles].

DASHWOOD, J. R.:
The falsification of the Royal Arch
Chapter of Compact. AQC Vol. 64
(1951).

FREEMASON (THE) AND MASONIC
ILLUSTRATED.
22nd July 1933, Special
Commemoration Number. Masonic
Peace Memorial. [Report of the
Dedication and description of the
building and its construction].

GILLEN, MOLLIE:
Royal Duke. Augustus Frederick, Duke of
Sussex (1773–1843). London, 1976.

HAUNCH, T. O.:
The Freemasons' Hall Medal of 1780.
AQC Vol. 82 (1969).
Freemasons' Hall Committee Token,
1778. AQC Vol. 89 (1976).

HEWITT, A. R.:
Recent notable additions to the Grand
Lodge Museum. AQC Vol. 80 (1967).

HEWITT, A. R. and GROVES, JOHN:
A selection of recent additions to the
Grand Lodge Library and Museum.
AQC Vol. 83 (1970).

HEWITT, A. R.:
The Supreme Grand Chapter of England.
A brief history from Lord Blayney to the
Duke of Sussex. London, 1966.
[Contains transcript of Charter of
Compact. An abbreviated version of
the paper (without the transcript)
printed as Appendix 'E' to Grand
Lodge, 1717–1967, q.v.]

JOY, E. T. and HEWITT, A. R.:
Some unrecorded Masonic ceremonial
chairs of the Georgian period. AQC
Vol. 80 (1967).

MANNERS, LADY VICTORIA:
Matthew William Peters, RA his life and
work. London, 1913.
[The Rev. Matthew William Peters
painted a number of portraits of Grand
Masters for the first Freemasons' Hall.
He was appointed Grand Portrait
Painter, a rank unique to him, in 1785].

MASONIC ILLUSTRATED
Vol. 1, No. 1, October 1900.
Freemasons' Hall – The New Wing
Vol. 1, No. 2, November 1900.
Freemasons' Hall – The Main Building
[Illustrated articles on the second
Freemasons' Hall at the turn of the
century]

POOLE, HERBERT S. [ED.]:
Gould's History of Freemasonry ...
revised, edited, and brought up to date.
4 vols. London, 3rd edition 1951.
[Volume 3 contains photographs of
complete text of the Articles of Union]

Quatuor Coronatorum Antigrapha [*QCA*]
Masonic Reprints of Quatuor Coronati
Lodge No. 2076, London:
Vol. x (1913) The Minutes of the
Grand Lodge of . . . England,
1723–1739
[Transcript with introduction and
notes by W. J. Songhurst]
Vol. xi (1958) Early Records of the
Grand Lodge of England according to
the Old Institutions
[Transcript with introduction by
J. R. Dashwood]
Vol. xii (1960) The Minutes of the
Grand Lodge of . . . England,
1740–1758
[Transcript with notes by W. J.
Songhurst edited by J. R. Dashwood]

SANDBY, WILLIAM:
*Thomas and Paul Sandby: some account
of their lives and works.* London, 1892.

STUBBS, SIR JAMES:
Major Portraits at Freemasons' Hall,
London. *AQC* Vol. 79 (1966)
Great Queen Street: Freemasons' Ha[ll]
and its environs. *AQC* Vol. 82 (1969)
Building a Temple, 1927–33. *AQC*
Vol. 89 (1976)

UNITED GRAND LODGE OF ENGLAND:
Grand Lodge 1717–1967. London,
1967.
[The 250th Anniversary History of
Grand Lodge; a symposium]

WILLIAMS, W. J.:
The Goose and Gridiron. *AQC* Vol.
(1924)

Ars Quatuor Coronatorum. [*AQC*]
Transactions of Quatuor Coronati Lodge,
No. 2076, London [Published annually].

Index[1]

ompiled by W. Bro. A. R. Hewitt, FLA, PJGD